LEADERSHIP DISCOVERY:

Journal & Resources for Growing Leaders

JANE MOYER

Published by New Century Leadership LLC, P.O. Box 223, Hinsdale, IL 60522

ISBN: 978-1-940975-07-8

CONTENTS

INTRODUCTION

Are you ready to unlock the full spectrum of your leadership potential? **"Leadership Discovery: Journal & Resources for Growing Leaders"** is designed to be your interactive guide and catalyst for growth.

The front half, the **"Journal,"** provides a space for self-examination, reflection, and goal setting as you explore your unique leadership style and potential. Use it to gather and develop significant ideas and record progress.

As you work through the Journal topics, use the companion **"Resources and Worksheets"** in the back half of the book in parallel. This section provides more detailed guidance, prompts, exercises, tools, and space to develop your Journal content.

Each segment of the book is designed to support you in exploring and addressing essential facets of your development as a leader:

Leadership Assets
No matter how far you are in your leadership journey, you bring many valuable assets to use. Exercises in the Resources section will help you discover and articulate them. Gathering your assets in one place in the Journal will bolster your confidence and help you be prepared to present yourself as a candidate when leadership opportunities arise.

Taking stock from time to time will help you acknowledge progress, recognize good-fit opportunities, and identify areas to expand further.

Leadership Purpose
In this segment, align your natural motivation and purpose with domains where you can make the most impact. Find the synergy between who you are and where you can lead most effectively.

Leadership Philosophy and Style
Draw inspiration from exemplary leaders to cultivate your leadership compass. This segment, coupled with **"Leadership Models"** in Resources, guides you in defining your leadership ethos and crafting a style that resonates with your principles.

Leadership Journey
Record your aspirations, plans, and milestones. Look ahead to **"Growing as a Leader"** in Resources for strategies to accelerate your leadership evolution.

Additional Resources on **"Leading Teams"** and **"Leadership Challenges & Skills"** provide insights and tools to help you master the nuances of leadership and rise to meet challenges with confidence and skill.

Welcome to "Leadership Discovery." Your journey to discover the leader within begins now.

LEADERSHIP
JOURNAL

LEADERSHIP ASSETS

STRENGTHS

VALUES

QUALITIES

SKILLS

EXPERTISE

EXPERIENCE

CONTRIBUTIONS

RESOURCES

RELATIONSHIPS & NETWORKS

Use the worksheets on pages 44–64 to discover and explore these assets. Then, summarize them here. Keep adding to them as you progress.

MY STRENGTHS

MY CORE VALUES

MY BEST QUALITIES

MY SKILL SETS

MY EXPERTISE

MY EXPERIENCE
Leadership, Work & Life

MY CONTRIBUTIONS

Contributions to organizations and projects that show my capabilities and readiness to contribute as a leader in the future

MY RESOURCES

Access to Information, Expertise, Technology, Tools, Funding, Facilities, Equipment, Lists, Audiences, Networks

MY RELATIONSHIPS & NETWORKS

Networks, Communities, Connections, Colleagues, Leaders, Followers, Collaborators, Customers, Resources, Advocates, Advisors, Allies, Models, Mentors, Support

LEADERSHIP PURPOSE

LIFE PURPOSE

SUCCESS CRITERIA

INTERESTS

DOMAINS & VISION

LEGACY

Use the worksheets on pages 65–69 to explore your purpose.

MY LIFE PURPOSE

Why am I here?

How can I keep this at the forefront of my thinking throughout my day?

MY SUCCESS CRITERIA

For me, success is ...

MY STRONGEST INTERESTS

WHY I WANT TO LEAD

MY LEADERSHIP DOMAINS & VISION

Where I aspire to lead and make an impact

Leadership Domain I:

How I could make a difference:

Needs and interests of potential Followers and Stakeholders:

My Vision for this domain:

Specifically, by the year _____, I'd like to see ...

Leadership Domain II:

How I could make a difference:

Needs and interests of potential Followers and Stakeholders:

My Vision for this domain:

Specifically, by the year _____, I'd like to see ...

Leadership Domain III:

How I could make a difference:

Needs and interests of potential Followers and Stakeholders:

My Vision for this domain:

Specifically, by the year _____, I'd like to see ...

MY LEADERSHIP LEGACY

What I would most like to be known and remembered for as a leader

LEADERSHIP PHILOSOPHY & STYLE

DEFINITION

MODELS

PRINCIPLES

INSPIRATION

CULTURE

Use worksheets pages 72-78, 80–81, and 100–108 as background for this section.

MY DEFINITION OF LEADERSHIP

MY LEADERSHIP MODELS
Style, qualities, actions, and contributions of leaders I admire

MY LEADERSHIP PRINCIPLES

LEADERSHIP INSPIRATION & QUOTES

THE LEADER I AM NOW

Where do I formally lead now?

Where do I lead informally now?

What are my standards as a leader?

How would I describe my leadership style now?

How might an observer describe my leadership style?

How might a follower describe my leadership style?

THE LEADER I WANT TO BE

FOLLOWERS

Whom do I aspire to lead?

What is important to them?

What impact would I like to have on them?

Why should they follow me?

LEADERSHIP & CULTURE

In what type of environment could I and my followers do our best work?

How could I create that culture?

MY LEADERSHIP JOURNEY

EXPERIENCE

OPPORTUNITIES

LEARNING

NETWORKS

For ways to accelerate your journey, see pages 144–161.

MY LEADERSHIP EXPERIENCE
Experiences I Can Draw Upon

Experience	What I did	What I learned

LEADERSHIP OPPORTUNITIES

MY LEADERSHIP LEARNING STRATEGY

Leaders are Learners.

Why, what, how, and when do I want to learn?

How can I accelerate my learning to grow as a leader?

MY LEADERSHIP NETWORKS

How will I continue to expand my network as I grow as a leader?

Who ...

   ... might I call upon for support?

   ... would inspire?

   ... could I learn from?

   ... might I call upon for advice?

   ... might be a good ally?

   ... might I collaborate with?

   ... might I serve?

   ... might I mentor?

What organizations, communities, or networks ...
    ... might be a good fit with my interests and capacities?

    ... might provide growth opportunities?

    ... might I be able to make a solid contribution to?

RESOURCES & WORKSHEETS

LEADERSHIP ASSETS & PURPOSE

STRENGTHS

VALUES

QUALITIES

SKILLS

CONTRIBUTIONS

PURPOSE

SUCCESS

RECOGNIZING YOUR STRENGTHS

Each of us possesses a unique combination of strengths—qualities, aptitudes, and skills in which we excel. These strengths include Natural Strengths—ones we are "born with," as well as Developed Strengths—ones we have developed through education or experience. Your strengths also likely include what you love to do, since we almost always enjoy doing what we are good at!

Three general methods of exploring your strengths are 1) Self-Evaluation, 2) Assessments, and 3) Feedback. Use a combination of these methods to uncover the fullest view of your strengths.

Self-Evaluation
What do you consider to be your strengths?
* *What do you think you do well?*
* *What comes easily to you?*
* *What do you notice or pay attention to that others don't?*
* *When have you been most successful?*
* *What sets you apart and makes you unique?*
* *What special expertise and talents have you developed?*

Assessments
Formal assessments can provide additional perspective on strengths. Examples:
* The Clifton StrengthsFinder® is an assessment developed by Donald Clifton and his colleagues at The Gallup Organization that identifies your five areas of greatest talent among 34 profile areas.
* The *Myers Briggs Type Indicator*® identifies your most natural ways of thinking and acting—how you get energy, what you notice first and most, how you approach decisions, and how you organize your life. A good interpretation of this assessment will include the identification of probable natural strengths and contributions.

Feedback

Feedback from others can be invaluable. Sometimes, we miss seeing our strengths because they are so natural to us that we assume they are also natural to everyone else.

* *What have your managers, teachers, or coaches identified as strengths?*
* *What have others told you, "Oh, you're so good at ..."?*
* Ask friends, colleagues, and family members what they think your strengths are.

STRENGTHS SELF-EVALUATION

Take stock of your strengths. Reflect on both personal and professional strengths. Consider both natural strengths and strengths you have worked to develop. Acknowledge your best aptitudes, skills, and qualities.

What do you think you do well?

What comes easily to you?

What do you notice or pay attention to that others don't?

When have you been most successful?

What sets you apart and makes you unique?

What special expertise and talents have you developed?

STRENGTHS FEEDBACK

What have your managers, teachers, or coaches identified as strengths?

What have others told you, "Oh, you're so good at ..."?

Ask 3–5 people who know you well in different contexts what they think your strengths are. For instance, you might ask a family member, a teacher or mentor, a manager, a coach or teammate, or a close friend. Listen carefully, ask clarifying questions if needed, and note their responses, paying particular attention to the words they use to describe your strengths.

DEVELOPING STRENGTHS

Take these steps to develop your strengths:

Recognize

The first step in developing your strengths is recognizing them. People are often surprised when others compliment them on their strengths. Because strengths are often natural talents or developed skills that come fairly easily, the talented one often doesn't recognize the talent as anything unusual. Their reaction is, "Doesn't everyone do that?" or "I thought everyone knew that."

Analyze

Specific identification and acknowledgment of strengths build confidence. Figure out how your strengths work. Step back and ask yourself:
- *How exactly do I do that?*
- *What's unique about the way I do that?*
- *How can I replicate that or teach it to others?*

Manage

Once you recognize how you operate using your strengths, you can regulate when and how you use them. Notice where and how you can contribute through your strengths. Avoid overusing them or applying them in inappropriate situations. Recognize when others might need you to slow down, explain, or give an example of things that seem easy to you but might not be to them.

Develop

Continue to build on your strengths through additional related education and experience.

Leverage

Look for opportunities to employ your strengths. Using your strengths allows you to shine. Develop a "personal brand" by becoming known for your unique combination of strengths.

Thrive
According to research by The Gallup Group, workers who get to use their strengths are significantly more engaged at work.

Bring Weaknesses Up To Required Standards
Generally one can get a better and faster "ROI," return on investment, by developing strengths rather than by shoring up weaknesses. However, some deficiencies can't be ignored. Know what's essential in your role and the roles to which you aspire. Work to bring required weak skills up to standards.

Additionally, consider alternative strategies for less strong or non-preferred functions. For instance:
- **Creating a System:** Could you, with help if needed, create a system to handle the function under most circumstances? For instance, could you create a template, formula, or process that works well without much or any effort on your part?
- **Partnering:** Could you collaborate with someone else who is strong in that area?
- **Delegating:** Could you delegate a significant part of the function?
- **Outsourcing:** Could you hire a third party with specific expertise to perform the function?

LEVERAGING YOUR STRENGTHS

Top strengths you have identified:
- Analytics
- Achievex
- Command
- Focus
- Relator

Where and how do you currently use these strengths?

I use mostly the analytics because in most situations I find myself in, I try to calculate & understand the pros & cons before making a decision. And I am an achiever that's why I keep chasing my dreams even when it starts feeling like a delusion

What opportunities exist for you to exercise and contribute your strengths?
For instance ...   In my day to day life

... on the job

... in your organization

... in your community

... in your family

What could you do to develop these strengths further?

Keep practicing & understands what makes me uncomfort-
& how to build on that

How aware are others of these strengths? If they're not already, how could
they become aware?

I think they are aware

PERSONAL VALUES
The Key to Sustainable Motivation
"Values are like fingerprints. Nobody's are the same, but you leave 'em all over everything you do." – Elvis Presley

Your Personal Values are:
- The ideals underlying what you care deeply about
- The basis of who you are when no one is looking
- The drivers of what you are naturally inclined to do
- Principles and qualities you treasure

Values are ...
- **Chosen:** While your background, parents, environment, and other factors may influence your values, you choose them yourself.
- **Constant:** Certain values may come to the forefront at different times and stages of life; however, your fundamental values don't usually change. Your values may become clearer through experience and focus.

Our awareness of values may become obscured by needs, "shoulds," obligations, environment, and other influences.

Values are <u>not</u> ...
- **... the same as Needs.** Needs are required, while Values reflect what we love and must have to live *optimally*.
- **... "Shoulds."** "Shoulds" reflect the opinions and needs of others. Values are our own.
- **... the same as Standards.** Standards are how you choose to behave. Values are not always acted on.
- **... always conscious.** If one has not deliberately examined their values, a first reaction is often to think values are what parents, teachers, religions, or other influential people or organizations have told us we "should" think is important.

Importance of Values:

- Values are the key to sustainable motivation.
- Values are the lens through which you make judgments.
- Identifying and prioritizing your values can facilitate decision-making and reduce internal conflict. Knowing your values can help you stay grounded during times of tumult.
- Shared values can be an important factor in successful long-term relationships.
- Recognizing others' values is a key factor in leading, managing, and influencing effectively.

Explore Your Values

- Intentionally reflect on your values.
- To identify your top values, consider:
  - *What matters most to you?*
  - *What "gets you going," either with enthusiasm or anger? (Your value is likely to be the reverse of the latter.)*
  - *What drives you to "go above and beyond"?*
- Values may "compete." Experiment with prioritizing your values.
- Make distinctions between related values (e.g., Honesty vs. Integrity).
- Look for evidence of your top values in your life.
- Ask someone who knows you well to tell you what they think your values are.
- Look for ways to design your life around your values.
- Watch for clues to other people's values. Listen deeply, but most importantly, watch what they do.

Know Your Values, Know Your Value

EXPLORE YOUR VALUES

Values are ideals that are personally important and meaningful for you. Examples of values are listed on the next page.

Identify ten values that are important to you. If you don't see one of your values listed, write it in.

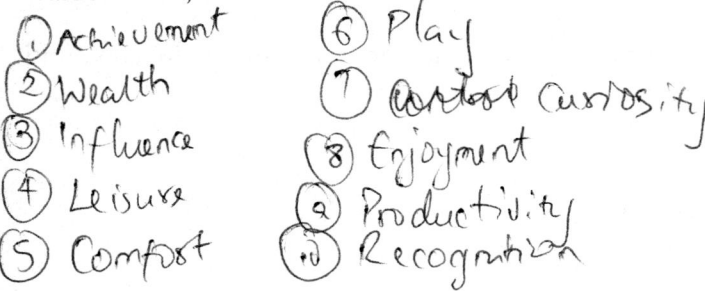

1) Achievement
2) Wealth
3) Influence
4) Leisure
5) Comfort
6) Play
7) Contact Curiosity
8) Enjoyment
9) Productivity
10) Recognition

Then select 3–5 top values from these. What's your #1 value?

My Top Values

1) Achievement

2) Wealth

3) Leisure

4) Enjoyment

5) Comfort

Achievement	Meaning	Competition
Sincerity	Balance	Faith
Creativity	Recognition	Courtesy
Progress	Logic	Fame
Power	Comfort	Contribution
Enjoyment	Beauty	Loyalty
Helping Others	Challenge	Order
Fairness	Security	Integrity
Knowledge	Honesty	Physical Skill
Stability	Individuality	Wisdom
Practicality	Competence	Discipline
Compassion	Tradition	Tolerance
Temperance	Leisure	Health
Humor	Justice	Self-Actualization
Reliability	Excitement	Respect
Excellence	Freedom	Service
Equality	Discovery	Control
Reciprocity	Family	Community
Wealth	Nurturing Others	Trust
Affiliation	Flexibility	Originality
Privacy	Prestige	Inner Harmony
Appreciation	Love	Reason
Responsibility	Learning	Friendship
Harmony	Cooperation	Play
Variety	Productivity	Independence
Spirituality	Relationship	Peace
Influence	Inspiration	Adventure
Teaching	Curiosity	

QUALITIES

While hiring managers typically focus on a candidate's knowledge, skills, and abilities, our personal qualities are often equally or even more important in determining ongoing success in our careers and lives. Examples of these qualities are listed on the next page. Add your own if you don't see them listed here.

What do you think your best qualities are?

I'm ... Calm
Supportive
Open Minded
~~Always~~ Productive

What good qualities have others acknowledged you for?

Oh, you're so ... Calm
Gentle
Supportive

What good qualities do you want to bring out?

Caring
intelligent
consistent

Accurate	Flexible	Open-minded
Adaptable	Focused	Optimistic
Adventurous	Fun	Orderly
Agreeable	Generous	Original
Alert	Genuine	Outgoing
Approachable	Gentle	Passionate
Articulate	Good-natured	Patient
Artistic	Gracious	Perceptive
Assertive	Helpful	Persistent
Authentic	Honest	Personable
Bold	Hopeful	Persuasive
Calm	Humane	Practical
Caring	Humble	Precise
Charming	Humorous	Prepared
Cheerful	Idealistic	Productive
Clever	Imaginative	Profound
Compassionate	Impartial	Progressive
Confident	Inclusive	Purposeful
Considerate	Independent	Quiet
Consistent	Industrious	Quick
Creative	Innovative	Rational
Curious	Inquisitive	Reasonable
Decisive	Insightful	Receptive
Dedicated	Inspirational	Reliable
Deep	Intelligent	Resilient
Dependable	Intentional	Resourceful
Diligent	Introspective	Responsive
Diplomatic	Intuitive	Sensible
Direct	Joyful	Sensitive
Discerning	Just	Sincere
Disciplined	Kind	Spontaneous
Dynamic	Level-headed	Strong
Efficient	Logical	Supportive
Eloquent	Loving	Tactful
Energetic	Loyal	Thoughtful
Enterprising	Masterful	Tolerant
Enthusiastic	Methodical	Tough
Expressive	Motivated	Vibrant
Fair	Nurturing	Warm
Fearless	Objective	Wise
Firm	Observant	Witty

SKILLS INVENTORY

Technical & Specialty Skills

What can you do or produce? What particular expertise or knowledge do you have? This includes specific knowledge or skills in areas such as Finance, Sales, Marketing, Law, Technology, Research, Engineering, Manufacturing, Construction, Healthcare, Human Resources, Operations, Education, Social Media, the Arts, and specific industry knowledge.

Thinking Skills

These skills provide an essential foundation for other skill categories.

Strategic Thinking

Analytical Thinking

Systems Thinking

Diagnostic Thinking

Design Thinking

Problem-Solving

Creative Thinking

Synthesis

Ethical Reasoning

Making Distinctions

Making Decisions

Generating Ideas

Evaluating Ideas

Managing Your Own Morale

Learning

Interpersonal & Communication Skills

This category includes a range of important career skills used to actualize other skills and to be effective in organizations.

Listening

Questioning

Writing

Speaking

Presenting

Making Proposals

Recommending

Giving Feedback

Persuading

Explaining

Validating

Requesting

Summarizing

Directing

Acknowledging

Supporting

Counseling

Contracting

Navigating Disagreement

Leading Meetings

Facilitating

Collaborating

Influencing

Building Relationships

Building Trust

Negotiating

Influencing

Connecting

Reading People

Bringing Out the Best in Others

Management Skills

These are activities and skills related to "getting things done," "doing things right," organizing, controlling, and implementing. They often involve processes, information, and defined timeframes.

Personal Productivity
Planning
Prioritizing
Administering
Implementing
Organizing
Controlling
Budgeting
Forecasting
Scheduling

Regulating
Supervising
Delegating
Hiring
Performance Planning
Setting Expectations
Developing Systems & Processes
Managing Projects
Managing Processes
Improving

Leadership Skills:

These are skills related to creating vision, "doing the right things," inspiring others, connecting, initiating, and changing. They often involve people, ideas, and the future.

Recognizing Trends
Anticipating Opportunity
Identifying Problems
Envisioning the Future
Creating a Shared Vision
Establishing Direction
Initiating
Leading Change
Giving Meaning
Innovating
Spotting and Attracting Talent
Developing Talent
Empowering Others

Inspiring Trust
Building Effective Teams
Creating Organizational Culture
Motivating
Coaching
Influencing
Balancing Diverse Needs &
    Perspectives
Building Support
Building Partnerships
Representing the Organization
Establishing High-level Relation-
    ships

STRONGEST SKILLS

Select your strongest five skills from your Skills Inventory. Then, note specific examples of how, when, and where you've demonstrated each skill.

Skill:
Experience, Examples & Evidence:

Skill:
Experience, Examples & Evidence:

Skill:
Experience, Examples & Evidence:

Skill:
Experience, Examples & Evidence:

Skill:
Experience, Examples & Evidence:

IDENTIFYING YOUR CONTRIBUTIONS

"The critical question is not "How can I achieve?" but "What can I contribute?"
—Peter Drucker

Identify ways you have contributed to your team, organizations, or communities. Look for contributions that are significant and, if possible, quantifiable or observable.

Responsibilities: Start by spelling out responsibilities you have had in positions you've held:
- *What has been the **scope** of your responsibility (e.g., area, production, revenue, customers, etc.)?*
- *What **results** have you been responsible for?*
- If you have held management responsibility, note the size of your staff and budgets.

Roles: In addition to your defined responsibilities, what other roles, if any, have you taken on and why? For example:
- *Chosen to represent a group, participated in a task force, elected to a board position, volunteered for a role, etc.*

Recognition: What have you been recognized for by others and why? Examples:
- *Awards*
- *Testimonials*
- *Promotions*

Results: What results have you produced that exceed the norms? For instance, look for stand-out results such as these:
- ★ *Improved outcomes*
- ★ *Fixed something or solved a difficult problem*
- ★ *Invented, created, or initiated something*
- ★ *Affected a change for the better*

* ★ *Accomplished more*
* ★ *Accomplished more with fewer resources*
* ★ *Increased something important (e.g., participation, efficiency, sales, revenue, production, ranking, retention, audiences)*
* ★ *Decreased something important (e.g., errors, customer complaints, downtime, expenses)*
* ★ *Saved time and/or money*
* ★ *Wrote, published, designed, or produced something*
* ★ *Achieved a record or did something for the first time*
* ★ *Developed a new system*
* ★ *Created a new community*

Write out your contributions as concisely and specifically as possible:
* Answer: *How? How much? Compared to what?*
* Identify your role.
* Translate contributions into quantifiable results (e.g., revenue, savings, scores, participation rates) or observable examples.
* Provide perspective (e.g., % increase or decrease, scale or rank, comparison to norms).

LIFE PURPOSE: CLUES

Your purpose is your reason for being—why you're alive and what you're here to do. Use these questions to explore and help you define your life purpose.

Your Natural Motivation
- *What do you love to do?*
- *What type of play did you enjoy most as a child?*
- *When have you persisted through difficult challenges when most people would have given up or settled for less?*
- *When have you taken on responsibility or work that wasn't required? Why did you put in the extra effort?*
- *When have you felt "in the zone"? What have you lost track of time or sense of self while doing?*
- *If finances or other responsibilities weren't a factor, what would you most like your life work to be?*

Your Treasure
- *What are your highest values?*
- *Of which accomplishments in your life are you most proud?*
- *When have you taken the strongest stand?*

Your Gifts
- *What are your natural strengths and talents?*
- *When have you felt absolutely at your best at work or play?*
- *What can you easily do that others can't?*

Your Uniqueness
- *What is unique about you?*
- *What are you known for?*
- *What do you pay attention to or notice that others don't?*
- *What have you done that no one else could have done so well?*
- *What "special sauce" do you delight in adding to your work?*

Your Legacy

- *Whom would you most like to serve? Why?*
- *How will you help them?*
- *What would you most like to be remembered for?*

HOW DO YOU DEFINE SUCCESS?

To me, "success" means ...

I have been successful in my life when I ...

When I am successful, I ....

To consider myself more successful, I ...

What would "success" look like for me?

What would "success" feel like?

What would it sound like?

To be more successful, I might need to ...

  ... do more of ...

  ... be willing to ...

  ... be ...

  ... give up ...

  ... change ...

CATHEDRAL BUILDING: WHAT I REALLY DO

Reflect on your greatest strengths, strongest interests, best skills, and favorite career activities. Is there a theme?

Think broadly. Think BIG. Think beyond yourself and day-to-day. What do you *really* do?

Remember the story of the two workers hauling and chiseling stone in Renaissance-era Italy. When asked what they were doing, one answered, "I'm cutting and laying stones," while the other replied, "I'm building a cathedral."

As you consider your career activities, shift into "cathedral building" mode.
- Look beyond the literal description of your activities. *What do they symbolize?*
- Look for patterns and meaning. *What's the greater purpose or idea tying your strengths and interests together?*
- Take it to a higher level. *Why is what you do important? How do you best serve others?*

Boil it down. Use just 2-4 words:
- An "action" word, and
- Where, how, or to what you apply it

Some examples: *I ...*
- *Turn Chaos into Order*
- *Solve Complex Problems*
- *Cultivate Talent*
- *Create Beauty*
- *Challenge Conventional Thinking*

What do you really do?

LEADERSHIP MODELS

MODELS

INFORMAL LEADERS

LEADERSHIP ROLES

LEADER BEHAVIORS

LEADER QUALITIES

MY LEADERSHIP MODELS

<u>Leader I Admire</u>   <u>Why</u>

OBSERVATIONS: INFORMAL LEADERS

Managers usually have titles that acknowledge their position and authority. Leaders may lead informally through influence.

As you go about your work, activities, classes, and life this week, watch for individuals who influence others positively and are good at getting things done without having formal leadership positions, titles, or authority. Notice how they lead in informal ways.

What Works

Notice how they get things done:
- *What do they do?*
- *Why do people respond?*
- *What else strikes you?*

Examples:

When you need to get things done without having formal authority, what behaviors, tactics, messages, or ideas could you adopt or adapt?

What Doesn't Work
Also, notice behaviors that are not effective.
* *What doesn't work?*
* *Why?*
* *What will you avoid?*
* *What else strikes you?*

Examples:

Takeaways
How might this apply to you and what you are aiming to achieve?

A LEADER'S ROLE

In "The Eighth Habit," Stephen Covey points out that "leadership is the highest of the arts, simply because it enables all other arts and professions to work." Leaders create vision and meaning; they connect and move people and ideas.

Management guru Warren Bennis distinguishes between the roles of Leader vs. Manager this way: "Leaders are people who do the right thing. Managers are people who do things right." Further, he notes, "Management is getting people to do what needs to be done. Leadership is getting people to *want* to do what needs to be done. Managers push. Leaders pull. Managers command. Leaders communicate." In practice, both roles are needed, and one person often plays both roles. For instance, there must be a vision; the vision then needs to be carried out in practical ways.

Roles of Leaders	Roles of Managers
• Visionary	• Organizer
• Architect	• Implementer
• Strategist	• Planner
• Influencer	• Supervisor
• Unifier	• Administrator
• Communicator	• Commander
• Connector	• Controller
• Motivator	• Resource Allocator
• Innovator	• Regulator
• Change Agent	• Forecaster
• Developer	• Evaluator
• Transformer	• Transactor

A Manager's power and authority typically come with a position and title. A Leader's power, however, comes largely through influence and trust, whether or not there is a title or formal position, so leaders can emerge from anywhere within an organization.

OBSERVATIONS:
LEADER BEHAVIORS

Watch effective leaders in action and note their behaviors.
What do they DO to move people and ideas ahead?

OBSERVATIONS:
LEADERSHIP QUALITIES

What qualities do you notice or admire most in leaders?

LEADING TEAMS

PROCESSES

ROLES

GOALS

DECISIONS

MEETINGS

RESOURCES

ORGANIZATIONAL VALUES

ORGANIZATIONAL CULTURE

BRINGING OUT THE BEST

OBSERVATION:
TEAMS THAT WORK

As you go about your work and life this week, watch for any type of high-performing team—whether it's a business team, a sports team, or a musical group.

Teams That Work

What makes the team successful? Notice:
- The Leader's character and behaviors
- Composition of the team
- How the Leader and Team Members work together
- Structure or processes contributing to their success

What else strikes you?

What behaviors, tactics, messages, or ideas could you adopt or adapt when building and leading a team?

What Doesn't Work

Also, notice poor-performing teams.

- *What doesn't work?*
- *Why?*
- *What will you avoid?*
- *What else strikes you?*

Briefly Stated...

Sum up each key discovery from your observations in one sentence (or even better, in *Just. Three. Words.*)

-

-

-

-

-

GETTING THINGS DONE: TEAM PROCESSES

Processes are HOW things get done in organizations. They address issues such as, "What methods do we use?", "Who is included?", "Where does accountability lie?", and "What order do we take things in?", which play a part in a team's efficiency, morale, and quality of work. Well-designed processes provide clarity, set proper expectations, prevent having to "recreate the wheel," and increase members' commitment.

While processes may be considered largely the province of Managers, there is overlap for Leaders. It's important to choose the right amount and the right type of processes to match your team's mission and culture. The right amount of effective processes can simplify, streamline, bring out solutions, and produce better results. For instance, the practice of sending agendas out before meetings allows participants to come well-prepared. Skillful ideation processes can produce a greater quantity and quality of ideas. Team members who have a say will likely be more committed to decisions. Conversely, too much or poorly designed process can clog the pipeline, create a frustrating bureaucracy, and suppress creativity.

Several process categories are listed on the next page. Rate relevant processes for your team.

Which processes are working well?

Which processes could be improved, clarified, or simplified?

What, if any, other processes could be beneficial?

Processes	n/a	Poor	OK	Good
Strategic Planning				
Operational Planning				
Communication & Information Sharing				
Meetings				
Decision-making				
Goal Setting & Prioritization				
Recruiting & Hiring				
Onboarding				
Assigning Responsibilities				
Managing Resources				
Measuring Progress				
Evaluating Performance				
Recognizing & Rewarding Success				
Training & Development				
Innovation				
Handling Disagreements				
Other:				

DEFINING ROLES

Clarity on roles and responsibilities within a team improves productivity, accountability, relationships, collaboration, and engagement.

List all the significant Functions and Responsibilities of your Team:

Then, list the available Team Members. Note their strengths, skills, interests, and other relevant factors that play into their capability and motivation to perform the functions successfully.

Then, define Roles (positions) and Responsibilities (functions, duties, tasks, expected results) by matching Functions and fitting Team Members.

Tips:
- Aim for balanced workloads.
- Define responsibilities so they are clear to both the assigned Team Member and others on the team.
- Note accountability. To whom does this person report? Who else relies on them? If helpful, draw a diagram showing responsible team members' relationships to each other.

Team Member	Role	Accountable To	Responsibilities

Revisit this from time to time to assess how it is working and adjust as appropriate.

GOAL SETTING

Goal:

Roles:

- Who will set the goal?
- From whom will they solicit input?
- What information and resources will be used?
- Who is responsible for achieving the goal? (If multiple people, define the role of each.)

Timeframe/Progress Points:

Measure(s) of Success:

Significance of Reaching Goal:

Potential Obstacles/Solutions:

Resources:

Action Plan:

Action Step	Person Responsible	Timeframe	Measure of Success

DECISION-MAKING PROCESS
Deciding How We Will Decide: Two Factors—Who and How

Who Will Decide?
The first factor in group decision-making is determining who will be involved in making the decision.

The Case for Inclusion: There may be a strong case for letting those who will be affected by a decision or involved in implementing it have a say. Involving more participants can increase commitment and produce a wealth of ideas.

The Case for Efficiency: The difficulty in reaching a decision grows exponentially as more decision-makers are involved. It's been said that "a camel is a horse designed by a committee." Trying to please everyone doesn't necessarily produce the best overall decision.

The choice of whom to involve may depend on the importance of the decision, the amount of input needed, and the level of commitment required. Einstein's advice may be a good guideline: *"Everything should be made as simple as possible, but not simpler."*

See additional notes on decision-making in large groups of equal decision-makers at the end of this section. (Yes, democracy can be messy.)

Decision-Making Roles
Owner: Every decision needs an Owner, the person ultimately responsible for it.

Approval: If approval(s) will be needed for your decision, determine the criteria for approval upfront.

Agreement: If the decision requires the agreement of multiple decision-makers, determine upfront the criteria each will use to decide. Keep in mind that the time and sub-agreements required may increase exponentially as the number of decision-makers increases.

Input: Gather information, solicit opinions and ideas, explore interests and needs, consider multiple perspectives, and build support by asking for input from stakeholders who will be affected by the decision (e.g., implementers, resource providers, potential customers.) Ask for input only if you will genuinely listen to it. Be clear that, while asking for individual input, many factors may influence your ultimate decision. Specify the type of input you are seeking.

Notice: Determine who needs to be informed of your decision afterward, as well as the best way and timing of communicating it.

Note: For complex decisions, Approval, Agreement, Input, or Notice may be needed for only parts of it.

Use the exercise on the following page to develop decision-making processes for your team.

How Will We Make Decisions?

List decisions that will need to be made by you and your team members.

Designate the person responsible for the decision as the **Owner.** Then, note the level of involvement needed from others:

- **Input:** The Owner seeks perspectives and information from others but still makes the final decision.
- **Agreement:** The Owner seeks agreement and/or cooperation before making the final decision.
- **Approval:** The Owner's decision requires approval from others.
- **Notice:** Others who need to be informed of the decision.

Decision	Owner	Input	Agree	Approve	Notice

Discuss the process with your team. Adjust as necessary. Implement the process and then review it occasionally to see how it's working and whether adjustments are needed.

DECISION-MAKING TOOLS
Seven Three-Step Decision-making Models
(Excerpt from *Leaders Lab: 66 Ways to Develop Your Leadership Skill, Strategy & Style* by Jane Moyer)

When you face decisions, consider using one or more of these simple three-step decision-making models.

1) **Head, Heart, Gut**
   Apply logic, feeling, and intuition by asking:
   - *What does your head say?*
   - *What does your heart say?*
   - *What does your gut say?*

   This method works well for personal decisions where there's more involved than facts. Get quiet and add a "gut" or intuition check along with facts and feelings. Notice whether love or fear is driving your decision. Are you reacting to the pressure of personalities or acting on principle? Are you open to new input or simply justifying your previous choices and actions?

2) **Best, Worst, Likely**
   Research by social scientists shows that people are more likely to act to prevent loss than to achieve gains. Some of us tend to optimistically focus on the "half-full" glass, while others first see the "half-empty" glass. Balance these tendencies by considering these three questions for each of your options:
   - *What's the best thing that could happen as a result?*
   - *What's the worst thing that could happen?*
   - *What would most likely occur?*

   For instance, in evaluating investments—what's the potential upside; what's the potential downside; what's most likely? Look to put your money on the option with the largest and likeliest upside and the smallest and least likely downside.

3) **Criteria Weighting**
   Most big decisions involve multiple factors. What's most vital in yours?
   1) Identify top criteria against which to evaluate your options.
   2) Prioritize your top criteria. What's most important of all?
   3) Weigh your options against your criteria, giving extra weight to the very top factors.

Decisions often require tradeoffs. For instance, in considering career options, one might face tradeoffs between factors such as compensation, preferred location, growth opportunities, fit with values, and work environment. Choices may be very personal. Identify what's most important to you and give that weight in your decision.

4) **3D Decision Making**
   Look at your options in three dimensions. For instance, evaluate how well your option would work:
   - Before/During/After
   - Short-term/Intermediate-term/Long-term
   - From 30,000 feet/On the ground/Under the microscope
   - For Shareholders/Customers/Employees
   - On a National/Regional/Local basis or
   - From an Operational/Financial/Sales perspective

5) **Kidder's Three Ways to Resolve Dilemmas**
   In his thoughtful book *How Good People Make Tough Choices*, Rushworth Kidder pointed out that decisions are often especially difficult when they involve choices between two types of good. For instance, in making a decision, one might need to weigh what's best for individuals versus what's best for the community or balance short-term benefits versus long-term ones. If you're facing this type of decision, he offers "Three Principles for Resolving Dilemmas":

- *"Do what's best for the greatest number of people."*
- *"Follow your highest sense of principle."*
- *"Do what you want others to do to you."*[1]

6) **De Bono's PMI: Plus/Minus/Interesting**

One of the most widely used decision-making methods is the "Pros and Cons" method attributed to Benjamin Franklin. In this method, one makes two columns on a sheet of paper, labels one "Pros" and the other "Cons," and then lists the pluses and minuses for each option under consideration.

Thinking expert Edward de Bono supplements this simple tool with a third column, "Interesting," where one lists other factors to consider. Doing so often opens up additional ideas and alternative solutions. Using this tool, then, one asks:

- *What are the pluses of this option?*
- *What are the minuses?*
- *What's interesting about it?*[2]

Don't be surprised if you generate better options using the process.

7) **Alternative Decision making**

We often get stuck thinking a decision means choosing between two (or more) prescribed options. *Yes/No. Either/Or. Black/White.*

Are you limiting yourself unnecessarily? Consider adding some color and stirring it up:

- **Think in broader terms:** What is it you're really after? If you think in broader terms, instead of either/or, you might be able to have both. For example, consider the saying, "You can't have your cake and eat it, too." What if you just wanted the memory of the cake? Take a photo and enjoy a slice.
- **Reframe:** Change the question and then look for an entirely different answer. Are you trying to decide between keeping your full-time job and being a stay-at-home mom? Instead, ask, "How

92

can I both contribute to family finances and have the flexibility to spend quality time with my kids?" That might open up an entirely new range of options, from job-sharing to entrepreneurship to a change of careers.

- **Flip a coin:** Can't decide? Don't want to? Maybe you don't have to. This doesn't mean avoidance, though; "Not to decide" is usually actually a decision to stay with the status quo. When any decision is better than no decision or an inconsequential choice simply has to be made, pick any method—even a random method like flipping a coin or throwing a dart. There, you've got a decision. Move forward, and don't look back.
- **Don't decide. Experiment:** You may come to a better decision if you play with it first. Before you lock in an important decision, try it out as an experiment, test, or prototype. When you see how it works out, your learning may lead to new ideas and alternatives, resulting in a better decision in the long run.

Large Groups of Equal Decision-makers

Voting as a Decision-making Method

When it is necessary to involve a large number of equal decision-makers, voting is the most efficient method. Voting, however, may not produce an ideal decision; nearly half of the voters may walk away unhappy. When making a group decision by voting, consider the following:

- Group members must agree to abide by the voting outcome.
- If there are more than two options, how many votes are required to "win" the vote? Is a plurality of votes—the most, but not a majority of votes cast—sufficient? If not, there may need to be a "run-off" to reach a majority of votes or the threshold sufficient to "win."
- Because voting doesn't provide an opportunity to negotiate or develop other options, an opportunity should be provided for open debate and discussion before voting.

Weighted Voting

When considering multiple options, weighted voting may produce a more satisfactory outcome. An example of how this might work: Decision-makers are given three "votes" to spread among multiple options as they choose. They might spread their votes out between three options or concentrate their votes on their most favored alternative.

Consensus Methods

Consensus methods often require a lot of time and patience, but present the possibility of higher-quality solutions to complex problems. Every group member agrees to support the decision, and they work together to develop the best option possible. They may use a secret ballot or straw poll to get a sense of how close they are to an agreement. They may ask hold-outs what they would need to make the solution acceptable. Ultimately, they may agree to a solution that is not ideal but is determined to be the best of imperfect options.

1. Rushworth Kidder, *How Good People Make Tough Choices: Resolving the Dilemmas of Ethical Living* (New York: Morrow, 1995).

2. Edward de Bono, *De Bono's Thinking Course* (New York: Facts on File, 1994), 12–19.

TEAM COMMUNICATION PROCESSES

Use this list of discussion topics as appropriate to your organizational responsibilities, structure, and culture to develop processes to streamline team communication.

Communication Preferences

While individual preferences may have to yield to group-wide needs and preferences, start by collecting contact information and finding out about individual communication preferences.

Preferred Contact Information
- Preferred Email
- Preferred Phone
- Other

Preferred Communication Methods
- Best Time/Way to Reach Me
- Timing Issues Affecting Scheduling/Contacts (e.g., if relevant, work hours, expectations/procedures (if applicable) for contact after work hours)

Team Communication Practices
- When Meetings are Needed
- Meeting Scheduling Procedures
- Virtual Meetings & Conference Call Procedures
- Meeting Protocol
- Email Practices (e.g., Subject Line conventions to signal response/action required and make them easy to find)
- Expectation re: Standard Response Time

- Accountability
  - How we'll handle things if no response is received
  - Procedure if one has to miss a call or meeting
  - Cancellations: Procedure/Notice
  - Rescheduling Responsibility
  - Responsibility/Procedure for providing information in advance
  - Responsibility/Procedure for obtaining missed information afterward

Information Sharing
- What information do Team Members need, and in what timeframe?
- What method is used to distribute information?
- Distribution Lists
- Confidentiality

SAMPLE MEETING AGENDA

Send out an agenda in advance of the meeting to give participants time to prepare.

Meeting Name:

Meeting Leader:

Meeting Date and Time:

Meeting Location:

Meeting Purpose:

Expected Outcome or Product:

Participants/Roles:

Preparation Required:

What to Bring:

Agenda Items	Person Responsible	Allocated Time

Contact for pre-meeting questions or suggested agenda additions:

RESOURCES

What resources are required for your team or project?
(e.g. Funding, Information, Technology, Materials, Equipment, Tools, Space, Services, Expertise, Support)

What other available resources could be helpful?

How will needed resources be obtained?

How will resources be allocated within the team?

What is the process to obtain team resources?

What accountability is built into the team's resource allocation and usage? (e.g., tracking, analysis or reporting, acknowledgment or reciprocation)

Sample Team Resources Plan

Project:

Determine resources needed. Then, identify potential sources, the process to access the resources, and accountability in using the resource.

Resources Needed:

Resource   **Source**   **Process to Access** **Accountability**

WORKSTYLE PREFERENCES
How do you do your best work?

	Your Preference	Others' Preferences

Energy
*What works best to help
you re-energize?*

Work Space
How important is ...
... privacy?
... quiet?
... social opportunity?

Productivity:
*How much do
interruptions bother you?*

Communication:
*Which do you prefer,
written or verbal
communication:*
*... when sending
information?*

*... when receiving
information?*

	Your Preference	Others' Preferences

Networking
What methods work best for you?

Learning
What methods work best for you?

Meetings
How important is notice/an agenda in advance?

What annoys you in meetings or keeps you from contributing your best?

Other Factors

ORGANIZATIONAL VALUES

Organizations embrace values that reflect **ends** (aspirations) and **means** (how things are accomplished).

What are your organization's major aspirations? Choose 1–3. (Add your own if needed.)

Aspirations (Ends): What to Be Known For

Industry Leadership	Size	Quality
Community Service	Marketing	Low Costs
Technical Leadership	Global Reach	Professionalism
Ethical Leadership	Service	Dependability
Customer Satisfaction	Specialization	Profitability
Social Responsibility	Fun	Innovation
Employee Satisfaction	Diversity	Sustainability

What values are revealed through how things are currently accomplished in your organization? What's emphasized and rewarded? Identify 5-10 top values. Then, choose three that are dominant.

How Things Are Accomplished (Means): Emphasis & Rewards

Fiscal Responsibility	Discipline	Punctuality
Achievement	Consistency	Implementation
Customer	Avoiding Mistakes	Protocol
Accountability	Courtesy	Candor

Learning	Diversity	Speed
Stability	Safety/Security	Risk-taking
Productivity	Integrity	Empowerment
Employee	Political Savvy	Connections
Salesmanship	Creativity	Loyalty
Competence	Expertise	Harmony
Winning	Teamwork	Individual
Fun	Trust	Service
Humor	Tact	Other:

How consistent are the values your organization demonstrates with the ones they state publicly?

Organizational values can change over time. For example, they might change due to:
- Change in leadership
- Change in markets
- Stage of product/lifecycle

How might your organization's values change in the future?

ORGANIZATIONAL CULTURE

"How Things Really Get Done Around Here"

What is expected ... What we believe ... How it works

Organizational Culture is reflected in Expectations, Beliefs, Norms, and Practices throughout the organization. It shows up in dimensions such as:

Power
- *How is power obtained? (e.g., through knowledge, position, contacts, financial resources, charisma, talent, etc.)*
- *What functions are considered most powerful?*
- *How are decisions made?*
- *How is access to resources determined?*

Values & Rewards
- *What do we pay attention to?*
- *What is valued? How does that show?*
- *What do we measure?*
- *What is rewarded? How?*
- *Who gets promoted? Why?*
- *Who are our heroes? Why?*
- *What and how do we celebrate?*
- *What stories do we pass down?*
- *How important is team participation and performance vs. individual performance?*
- *What are our beliefs about diversity, and how does that show?*
- *What do we believe about customers, and how does that show?*
- *How much emphasis is placed on competitiveness?*

Structure & Status
- *How is the "pecking order" determined?*
- *How strictly do we follow hierarchy?*
- *Who is included?*
- *Who participates?*
- *Who cooperates?*

- *How is status recognized?*
- *To what extent is individuality encouraged?*

Rituals & Protocol
- *How much formality is expected?*
- *How are meetings run?*
- *What is acceptable dress?*
- *What kind of work hours are expected?*
- *What are the expectations about socializing with colleagues outside of work?*
- *How much space do we give each other, literally and figuratively?*
- *What traditions are observed?*
- *How are we expected to show commitment?*

Time
- *What is our pace?*
- *What is our sense of urgency?*
- *How important is punctuality?*
- *Do we focus more on the short-term or long-term?*

Trust & Transparency
- *How much information is shared?*
- *How is it shared?*
- *What do we believe about each other's competence?*
- *How much do we trust our leaders, colleagues, employees?*
- *What subjects are taboo?*
- *What is hidden?*

Conflict
- *How are disagreements handled?*
- *How open are we to the expression of differing opinions?*
- *How open are we to discussing controversial issues?*
- *What happens when goals are missed?*
- *How do we handle mistakes?*
- *How much emotion is it acceptable to show?*

Change

- *How open are we to new ideas?*
- *How do we handle challenges to the status quo?*
- *How do we think about the future?*

Leaders often operate within a larger culture, such as a country's or large organization's culture, but also influence the culture of their own team, department, or program.

Aspects of organizational culture are sometimes obvious and sometimes subtle. To learn about an organization's culture, you might ask: *If you were giving honest advice to a new organization member on how to be successful here, what would you tell them?*

Be patient and persistent when attempting to change culture. It takes some time to break out of traditional thinking, patterns, and habits to establish new ones and trust in them.

Your Organizational Culture

Describe the Organizational Culture you operate in:

If a friend of yours were joining your organization, what advice would you give them about how things work?

What are some of the organization's "unwritten rules"?

Sum up the culture in a few key words (e.g. "Work Hard, Play Hard").

Creating Team Culture

As a Leader, within your realm, what culture will you create?

Describe your ideal culture in terms of:
- *Distribution of Power*
- *Rituals & Protocols*
- *Values & Rewards*
- *Pace*
- *Transparency*
- *Conflict*
- *Emphasis on the Individual vs. the Team*

Then, sum it up in a few key words:

If this culture is not the reality now, what could you do to move closer to it?

TEAM LEADERSHIP: BRINGING OUT THE BEST

Select motivated teammates who will be committed to your shared purpose. Get to know them, their strengths, values, interests, and what they need to do their best work.

Set your team up for success. Give team members a chance to know each other before taking on complex challenges together. Provide clarity on roles, success criteria, resources, and essential processes. Smooth the way.

Recognize and embrace the value of diverse backgrounds, perspectives, and styles.

As much as possible, give individuals assignments that interest them, capitalize on their strengths, and provide an opportunity to grow.

Ensure individuals understand the team goals and standards, their piece's importance, and how it fits into the whole.

Give team members a fitting combination of support (resources, information, direction, listening, coaching) balanced with freedom on how they accomplish the goal.

Measure, make visible, and reward the things that matter most.

Create a culture consistent with your goals and values that reinforces constructive behaviors. Model what you want.

Know when to lead. Know when to listen and adapt.

LEADERSHIP CHALLENGES & SKILLS

MINDSET

CONFIDENCE

VISIBILITY & POWER

INFLUENCE

TRUST

ASKING

LISTENING

IDEATION

PRESENCE

LEADERSHIP MINDSET

See what happens when you think of yourself as a Leader

If I thought of myself as a Leader, I would...

... pay attention to ...

... do more ...

... stop doing ...

... let go of ...

... change ...

... reach out to ...

... learn more about ...

... watch for ...

... guard against ...

... be bold about ...

THE CONFIDENCE TO LEAD

What might hold me back from leading or taking on new challenges?

How could I move forward?

Under what conditions would it be OK to quit instead?

What fears do I need to address?

How can I balance confidence with willingness to learn and listen to others?

What experiences could I pursue to increase my confidence in leading?

HANDLING VISIBILITY, PRESSURE, AND POWER

How will I handle the visibility that comes with being a leader?

While serving others, how will I maintain appropriate self-care, privacy, and space for reflection?

In my leadership role(s), what boundaries do I need to draw?

How will I stay true to my values and ethics?

How can I be wise to recognize and protect myself against attempts others might make to manipulate or use me?

How can I maintain a balance of appropriate humility and confidence?

What must I remember to be the person I want to be?

WHO HAS INFLUENCED YOU?

Think of someone who has had a significant influence on you.

Why were they, in particular, able to influence you?

What did they do?

What did it mean to you?

Would you accept their influence again?

If so, what makes you open to their ongoing influence? If not, why not?

What would the impact be if you could influence others in that way?

YOUR CAPACITY AS AN INFLUENCE FOR GOOD

*Influence: the capacity to have an effect on
the character, development, or behavior of someone or something*

Leaders think beyond themselves and today, putting themselves in a place to influence others for good.

When you seek to influence, first check your motives. Good influence reaches beyond personal gain and self to a greater good. Rather than manipulating or pressuring others to one's personal will by personal means, this type of influence comes from a leader at their highest and best, seeking to bring out the best for all concerned.

While we might first think of influencing as persuading and telling, effective influence comes as much by modeling, seeking understanding, asking, listening, and caring.

When you seek to influence, here's a good guideline from expert Robert Cialdini: *"Always be sure to influence another in a way that ensures that you haven't damaged your ability to influence this person again in the future. In other words, the other person must benefit from the change you've created."*[1]

Influence doesn't necessarily follow hierarchical lines of authority or titles. Some people achieve influence beyond their formal positions. People regularly turn to them for input and advice. Others seek them out to carry out important initiatives. They can often be identified by asking, "Who influences the decision-maker?" Sometimes, they are described with terms such as "the architect," "the brains behind ...," "an insider," or "a connector."

The amount of influence one wields is situational. It will change from opportunity to opportunity depending on many factors, including the level of expertise one has with a particular issue and their reputation with the players involved.

Factors that might determine and enhance one's level of potential influence include:
- **Position:** Role and responsibilities
- **"Track Record":** Past contributions and successes
- **Reputation:** What one is known for. Perceptions of one's competence and character.
- **Interpersonal Skill:** Ability to establish rapport, gain trust, and communicate effectively
- **Expertise:** Special knowledge and skill
- **Network:** Whom one knows and can easily call upon
- **Connections:** Power one can deliver through alliances, leverage, or inside knowledge
- **Resources:** Financial resources, information, equipment, tools, staff, and other resources
- **Other Value:** Other potential value the individual brings to a particular situation
- **Influence Characteristics:** Persuasiveness, negotiation ability, motivation, energy, appearance of success

Even more compelling may be factors that don't rely on past achievement or developed skills:
- **Trustworthiness:** Perception that one can be counted on to deliver, to keep confidence, to consider others' needs and interests
- **Inspiration:** Ability to articulate ideas that reach beyond one's self

What are your motives in trying to influence?

115

Where could you be an influence for good??

What characteristics do you demonstrate that could enhance your influence?

[1]Guy Kawasaki interview with Robert Cialdini: Book Review: *Influence-Science and Practice* - Guy Kawasaki. https://guykawasaki.com/book_review_inf/

YOUR INFLUENCE MAP

(Excerpt from *Leaders Lab: 66 Ways to Develop Your Leadership Skill, Strategy & Style* by Jane Moyer)

Draw an organizational chart indicating formal reporting relationships for your organization.

Now, think about how things *really* get done in your area. Draw a diagram showing whose involvement is needed to complete a significant project or make a major decision.

.

What, if any, difference is there between your two drawings?

To be effective in your organization, you will likely need to influence people with whom you have no formal reporting relationship. It will be important to build trust and support to move ideas and projects forward and get things done.

In addition to those you are formally related to on the organizational chart:
* *Whose help do you need to get important projects done?*
* *Who has expertise or special skills you'll need?*
* *Who has access to information and resources?*
* *Who can call upon a significant or influential network?*
* *Who is an "opinion leader" whose support can help move new ideas forward?*
* *Who is a "gatekeeper" who can say no or block critical access?*
* *Who has formal power (i.e., power because of position, title, etc.)?*
* *Who has informal power (i.e., power because of connections, track record, reputation, or style)?*
* *Who will evaluate your work?*
* *With whom would your boss say it is essential for you to have a relationship?*

Also, consider your influence on others:
* *Who has a stake in your success?*
* *Who needs your help to move their ideas and projects forward?*
* *With whom do you feel a natural connection?*

Now, draw your "Organizational Influence Map" on the next page.

Your Organizational Influence Map

Whose help, support, approval, resources, cooperation, attention, and trust do you need? Who needs yours?

Formal Power
Bosses, Subordinates

Resources
Information, Budget
Expertise, Network

Opinion Leaders
Connectors,
Influencers

You
Formal Power
Informal Power
Influence

Gatekeepers

Implementers

Customers

PREPARING PROPOSALS

Consider your audience's needs and preferences as you prepare proposals and presentations.

Needs & Interests

Business Needs:

Success Criteria:

Priorities:

Personal Needs:

Values:

Proposed Solution

Solution:

Benefits to Them:

Minimizing Their Risk:

Presentation Format
Practical Issues and Communication Preferences:

What Do They Focus on First and Most?
- Big Picture vs. Detail?
- Logic vs. People?
- Quick Closure vs. Alternatives?

What to Send in Advance:

21 INFLUENCE STRATEGIES

Pick Your Battles
Concentrate your influence efforts on issues of importance—not only to you, but to those you are attempting to influence.

Know "WHO" You Are Trying to Influence
Discover as much as possible about the person you are trying to influence. Find out what they value. Identify their needs, interests, and success criteria. Observe their style. Notice what they respond to and adapt. Accommodate their preferences if you can. Treat them the way they like to be treated. "Speak their language."

Cultivate a Reputation for Trustworthiness
Demonstrate competence, reliability, and character. Show consideration for others' needs and interests.

Show
Model what you want.

Show Up
Be present. Put yourself where the action is.

Show Up as an Expert
Build special expertise. Establish credibility by delivering results. Extend yourself as a resource in your specialty area.

Initiate
Make a request. Make a proposal. Make an offer. Put something out for others to respond.

Make It Easy
Make it easy for others to say "yes." Make your proposal attractive. Simplify. Limit choices. Eliminate objectionable or complicated details. Design a

system with a natural progression. Create an environment that supports the change you want.

Customize
Tailor messages and solutions to others' needs, wants, and situations so that benefits are clear.

Listen
Give the speaker your full attention. Listen for what's most important to them. Listen for understanding. Listen for what's being said and not said. Show others they've been heard.

Ask Skillful Questions
Seek understanding. Ask to obtain information. Ask to connect. Ask to uncover needs and discover interests. Ask to detect opportunities. Ask questions that lead to solutions.

Let Them Experience It
Make your solution visible. Apply it directly to their situation or show relatable examples. Give a sample. Let them see, hear, touch, and feel it.

Make It Their Idea
Ask for advice, help, input, and suggestions.

Take Away Fear
Do what you can to eliminate or diminish invalid fears. Aim for solutions that minimize risk or potential loss.

Jar Thinking
When stuck, shake up routine thinking with the unexpected. State a surprising fact. Reverse order. Come at it from the opposite direction. Use humor.

Give

Be the kind of person who gives first. Extend invitations and favors. Help others make connections. Share your good. Pay others back in ways that are meaningful to them. Pay it forward.

Go Social

Be likable. Build community. Find allies. Influence Influencers. Show that others already like you and your idea. Speak well of others and be appreciative when others speak well of you.

Appeal to Feelings

Consider and acknowledge likely feelings. Uncover and address fears. Show enthusiasm. Be authentic. Reveal your humanness. Connect through relevant personal stories.

Go Big

Agree on what the ultimate outcome will look like and work backward.

Go Small

Find small things you can agree on as a starting point. Establish some momentum and build from there.

Bring Out Their Best

Recognize the best in others, and it hold it out for them to step into.

TRUST BEHAVIORS

Trust is one of the most essential factors in influence and leadership. Rate yourself on the following behaviors that engender trust between individuals:

We Tend To Trust Someone Who:	Rate Yourself (1-5, 5 Highest)
Tells the truth	
Keeps their word	
"Walks their talk"	
Promises only what they can deliver	
Is fair and consistent	
Is competent in the area in which we are associating with them	
Gives appropriate credit to others	
Admits mistakes and accepts the consequences	
Tells us directly, not others, when we are doing something wrong	
Discloses their agenda and interests	
Defines expectations and communicates clearly	
Alerts us to risks that may affect us	
Seeks to understand others' viewpoints	

We Tend To Trust Someone Who:	Rate Yourself (1-5, 5 Highest)
Considers others' needs and interests as well as their own	
Shares important information and involves us in important decisions that affect us	
Doesn't surprise us with bad news or unpredictable behavior	
Influences us to act in ways that will make us successful	
Uses open body language	
Doesn't abandon us or their principles when times get tough	

Choose 1–3 behaviors from the above list to improve.

Actions to take:

POWER TOOLS: QUESTIONS

(Excerpt from *Leaders Lab: 66 Ways to Develop Your Leadership Skill, Strategy & Style* by Jane Moyer)

Questions are like power tools. They can get the job done faster and with less effort. Pick some up and learn to use them well.

Use The Right Tool for the Job
Recognize the difference between two basic question structures and when each works best:

> **Open Questions:** These are broad questions used to open conversations and identify a direction to pursue further. They usually start with *What, Why,* or *How* and encourage the other person to talk. For example:
> - *What would you like to achieve?*
> - *Why are you considering a change?*
> - *How can I help?*
>
> **Closed Questions:** These are focused questions used to obtain specific information. They usually start with words like *Who, Which, When, How Much,* or *Where* and can be answered in a few words. *Yes, no, blue, tomorrow, $100, Chicago, George.* For example:
> - *Do you like this?*
> - *Which color do you prefer?*
> - *When do you need it?*
> - *How much will it cost?*
> - *Where shall I send it?*
> - *Who needs to approve this?*

Notice how different types of questions are used for different purposes. For instance:
- **Diagnostic Questions** are used to obtain information, identify needs, and detect opportunities. *What are your concerns? What would be ideal? What would it take?*

- **Provocative Questions** challenge and stimulate thinking. *What's likely to happen if you do nothing? To what extent is x a problem for you? If there were a way to do y, would you be interested?*
- **Clarifying and Confirming Questions** ensure understanding. *If I understand correctly, you're looking for x—is that right? What exactly do you mean by "y"?*

Three Power Questions

Three simple but extremely powerful questions are:

Oh? Information is power. Find out more with a simple indication of interest and curiosity. *Mmmm. Tell me more. What else? Who else? How else?*

Why? Get to the root of the issue with a simple "Why?" Keep asking until you get there. To avoid sounding like a three-year-old, vary your subsequent whys slightly—*What do you hope to accomplish? What's your interest?*

How Might We ...? Generate solutions by directing thought to your desired outcomes. *How might we accomplish both x and y?*

QUESTION COLLECTION

Collect good questions for different purposes.

Opening Conversations

Solution-Finding

◯ What approach will you take to solve this?
◯ What's the first idea comes to you

Negotiating

Networking

Hiring

- How can you improve this Org.
- What are your Values
- Tell me about yourself
- What are your Personal Project

Coaching

- Whats your ~~experine~~ Experience?
- How can you contribute to the team values?
- How Can you improve the team spirit?

Collecting Feedback

- Whats your feed back?
- Whats your Opinion?
- Do you like this?
- ~~Do yo~~ - Anything else?

Strategy

Life

- How has life been?
- What makes life worth living?
- What are your life goals?

Favorite Questions

What?!!

LISTENING FOR UNDERSTANDING

Practice these listening skills and incorporate them into your interactions.

Restating: State it again. Use it to:
- Let them hear their own words.
- Emphasize a point.
- Encourage the speaker to refine or expand on their point.

Paraphrasing: Express the meaning in your own words. Use it to:
- Check for understanding.
- Turn a negative statement into a positive one.

Clarifying: Make a statement more comprehensible by asking for more information.
By that, do you mean ...? Would that include ..., then?

Confirming: Verify the correctness of your understanding.
If I understand you then, ...

Supporting: Affirm the speaker's comment.
I see what you're saying ... That's true. ... That's an important point ... I agree ...

Building: Acknowledge another's comment and add to it.
Yes, and ... Along with that ...

Probing for Understanding: Ask questions to increase your understanding.
Tell me more about that ... What's most important here? ... Could you give me an example?

Summarizing: Briefly state the main points.
To summarize, ... Recapping our discussion ... In a nutshell ...

Allowing Silence

FULL-BODIED LISTENING

(Excerpt from *Leaders Lab: 66 Ways to Develop Your Leadership Skill, Strategy & Style* by Jane Moyer)

Listen with your ears.
- Listen for the words and the message. Listen to all of it.
- What is the speaker's tone communicating?
- What is their pace telling you?

Listen with your head.
- Does what the speaker says make sense? Is it logical and consistent?
- Nod occasionally. In fact, nod three times. This encourages the speaker to continue. (Caution: Refrain from this in cultures or cases where it may be interpreted as an "I agree" nod instead of the intended "I'm listening" nod.)
- Resist letting other thoughts in (such as your planned response) while listening.

Listen with your eyes.
- Keep good eye contact.
- What signals do you notice from the speaker's body language and facial expression?

Listen with your heart.
- What's important to the speaker?
- What is their intention?
- What do they need?
- What do you have in common?
- What do you like about what's being said?
- Connect heart-to-heart.

Listen with your gut.
- What's the message behind the message?
- Can you trust the speaker?
- What opportunities are being presented?

- What's NOT being said?

Listen with your whole body.
- Give the other your full attention.
- Lean in a little.
- Listen while you speak, too.

BETTER BRAINSTORMING

(Excerpt from Leaders Lab: 66 Ways to Develop Your Leadership Skills, Strategy & Style *by Jane Moyer)*

Boost your brainstorming results by incorporating group and idea-generation best practices.

Draft a Potent Participant Combination
Select participants with contribution and collaboration in mind. Invite people with a genuine interest in the topic and motivation to find solutions. Include members with different experience, roles, and perspectives.

Keep the group to a size conducive to participation—usually eight or fewer. You'll want a group large enough to inspire a variety and volume of ideas, but small enough that participants feel their contributions are needed and important.

Consider changing the group membership occasionally to keep it fresh. For instance, bring in an expert or, conversely, bring in a smart, innovative person who knows little about your topic. It will be easy for them to get "outside the box" since they don't know where the box is.

For major brainstorming meetings, consider designating a Recorder to capture all the ideas and a Facilitator, whose role is to manage the process but not contribute ideas. A Facilitator sets up the space, manages the time, guides the group to work together effectively, uses tools to stimulate thinking, ensures that ideas are recorded, summarizes decisions, and obtains agreement on the next steps so you and your participants can focus on the creative part.

Lead With a Productive Question
Choose a topic that 1) warrants the group's time, 2) would benefit from a creative approach, and 3) is one you're likely to act on afterward. Pose a question that's broad enough to expand thinking, but specific enough to produce practical ideas. Ensure you're addressing the underlying issue by

articulating, "What we really want is... " Keep asking "Why?" until you get to the root reasons. Begin your brainstorming question with "How can we... ?" to open thinking. Circulate the central question in advance to allow people to mull it over.

Get Off To a Good Start
Set up for creative collaboration. A distraction-free space away from everyday tasks is ideal. Arrange the group in a semicircle facing "the problem" together. Allow room for participants to move around. Incorporate visuals and symbols to trigger humor, playfulness, and inspiration.

Warm up creative thinking with a funny cartoon or video about your topic. Provide materials to collect and develop ideas, including materials for individual use—paper, colored notecards, or "backs of envelopes"—as well as materials to build on others' ideas, such as colored markers, sticky notes, whiteboards, or flip charts.

You're probably familiar with the basic rules of brainstorming: 1) Go for a volume of ideas. 2) Anything goes. 3) Don't judge ideas yet. Briefly review these guidelines with the group.

To prompt a greater and faster flow of ideas, set goals (*Let's try to generate 20 ideas ...*) and time limits (*... in 10 minutes*). If you're in the midst of an idea cascade, you can always extend the time.

Individual Thinking First
To make the most of the group's collective thinking, begin with individual idea generation. Before opening up group discussion, give individuals a few minutes of quiet to think and jot down ideas. This helps quieter participants develop their ideas enough to speak up without getting drowned out by more extroverted types. It also prevents the capable but lazy from simply drafting on others' efforts. If there is a big difference in experience or level, ask the higher-ranking and more experienced participants to hang back initially to encourage others to contribute fresh and unbiased ideas.

Stimulate Ideas

Use creativity techniques to stimulate ideas:

Building: "Hitchhike" or "piggyback" on ideas already expressed. Create variations. Keep the conversation flowing with questions such as "What else could we do along the same lines?" or "What could be added or altered?"

Shifting: When building slows down, switch gears to go in a different direction. Ask, "How can we look at this differently?"

Restart: Pause, repeat, or reframe the question. Alternate between individual and group idea generation.

Improvise: Draw out ideas with an improviser's technique. No matter what the person before you says, say "Yes, and … "

Challenge assumptions: Identify and remove presumed limits.

Try on different hats: Look at your problem as different stakeholders or totally unrelated parties would. For instance, how would your customer or a five-year-old view your situation?

Ideas tend to come in bursts and improve as you go, so keep pushing to get past the obvious.

Make It Useful

Nothing is more demotivating to brainstorming participants than investing their time and energy and then seeing nothing happen as a result. Make sure to define and execute an appropriate follow-up process. For a simple issue, you might evaluate ideas immediately and make a decision. For more complex and vital issues, let the ideas simmer for a short time, provide a means to supplement them, and then get back together to refine, combine, cull, adjust, evaluate, and choose ideas for specific follow-up.

SHOWING UP AS YOUR BEST

The Impact of Nonverbal Communication

(Excerpt from *Leaders Lab: 66 Ways to Develop Your Leadership Skill, Strategy & Style* by Jane Moyer)

The Challenge: Making a Good Impression and Commanding Attention

As a leader of any kind, you'll be required to "show up" in front of others in a compelling, credible, and confident way, whether that involves speaking in front of a large group, directing a small group meeting, or communicating one-on-one.

Try This: Don't Neglect the All-Important 55%

First Impressions Count!

Social psychologists find that most people form initial impressions of each other within 5–20 seconds. This "first impression" is typically a "gut" reaction to nonverbal factors such as:

- Posture
- Body language
- Facial expression
- Gestures
- Eye contact
- Personal space
- Dress and appearance
- Tone of voice

The Impact of Nonverbal Communication: 55%

Even after this initial impression, these nonverbal factors play a significant role in personal effectiveness. According to UCLA Professor of Psychology Dr. Albert Mehrabian's famous study of *"Silent Messages,"* tone of voice and body language play a significant role in how much we like and believe a speaker. He found that, **when talking about feelings or attitudes, words alone account for only 7% of the speaker's likability, while tone of voice accounts for 38% and body language 55%.** Additionally, he found that if these elements aren't congruent, we tend to trust the nonverbal elements rather than the literal words.[1] Most of the time, the nonverbal message is expressed and interpreted subconsciously.

Interpretation of nonverbal communication can vary according to culture. The following suggestions are made for North Americans.

Posture: Posture particularly conveys confidence, energy, and interest. It reflects a combination of mental state and physical habit. Explore how posture changes based on your mental state. For example, note how your posture might change if you felt very proud versus depressed. Then, experiment with the reverse; explore how your mental state changes when you change your posture. Does a "power pose" make you feel more confident?

Generally, the most effective posture, both for speaking and for creating a solid impression, is straight, with shoulders slightly back but slightly relaxed. This creates an impression of confidence and credibility, while also allowing you to breathe deeply and speak with a strong, lower-pitched voice.

Body Language: Intentional or unintentional body movements, poses, gestures, and facial expressions may suggest mental states such as defensiveness, aggression, or nervousness; or suggest possible dishonesty, disinterest, or weakness. Notice your reaction to someone with:

- Slumped shoulders
- Fingers on lips
- Closed fist gestures
- Arms folded over chest
- A habit of fiddling nervously with accessories or clothing
- A limp handshake

According to body language experts, these all send signals that detract from one's power and message. For instance, closed fists or arms folded over the chest convey nervousness or defensiveness. Slumped shoulders and limp handshakes convey weakness. Fingers on your lips suggest you might be holding something back, and fiddling signals boredom.

Adopt more effective body language:
- Alert posture with head held high
- Standing straight when speaking; leaning forward slightly when listening
- Open body stance without crossed legs, feet, or arms
- Feet pointing where you want to go
- Arms slightly in front of you around waist level, with elbows bent or relaxed at your sides
- Palms up to convey openness; palms open toward yourself to draw others to your ideas; palms down to convey authority.
- Gestures that support your message
- Pleasant facial expression—a genuine smile, if appropriate
- Firm, but not crushing, handshake with good eye contact
- Hand offered with your palm in a vertical position to convey equality

Some body language experts suggest subtly mirroring the other person's body language.

Eye Contact: Eye contact can be used to:
- Establish or determine a level of trust.
- Check for understanding.
- Pick up nonverbal signals.

Good eye contact is needed to establish credibility. Eye contact that is too intense, however, can create distrust or discomfort. A suggested guideline is to maintain eye contact approximately 75% of the time while talking and listening.

Personal Space: Some individuals have a strong reaction to what they perceive as an invasion of their "personal space." While acceptable personal space can vary significantly by culture and individual, cultural anthropologist Edward T. Hall, known for his research on the effect of personal space in interpersonal communication, suggests these general guidelines for personal space:

- Intimate Distance: 6–18 inches
- Personal Distance: 1.5–4 feet
- Social Distance (appropriate for business interactions): 4–12 feet
- Public Distance (used for public speaking): 12 feet or more[2]

Dress and Appearance: Dress and appearance affect the perception of credibility, competence, and fit. Appropriate dress depends both on the culture and the specific situation. In general:
- Think "polished and professional."
- When in doubt, dress up.
- For interviews, dress for the position 1–2 levels above the one you are interviewing for.
- Avoid clothes or accessories that will distract from you and your message.
- Remember that accessories, such as a good briefcase or bag, portfolio, or writing pad and pen, are an important part of your appearance.

Vocal Power: Your voice also plays a vital role in how you and your message are received. To speak more powerfully using the lower part of your vocal range, stand tall, breathe deeply, and stay relaxed through your shoulder, neck, and throat areas. Vary your tone, volume, and pace to dramatize your message. Pause to let your message sink in.

Last Impressions Count, Too
Along with our first contact with someone, we tend to remember our most recent contact. Conclude your communication effectively, both verbally and nonverbally, whether it's with a handshake, a smile, or a confident walk.

Apply & Evaluate: What Do You Notice?
Observe influential leaders and pay attention to their nonverbal communication. (You might even turn down the audio while watching them on video.) Notice their posture and gestures:

- *How does their "look" affect your impression of them?*
- *How do they command attention? What type of posture and gestures are effective?*
- *What can you learn from them as you hone your presentation style?*

Take Action: Now What?

When you prepare to give a talk, run a meeting, or participate in a conversation, keep in mind the impact of nonverbal communication. Practice delivering essential messages in front of a mirror; or record and then watch yourself, paying attention to your posture, gestures, eye contact, and facial expression. Make an effort to create a solid first and last impression.

[1]A. Mehrabian, *Silent messages: Implicit communication of emotions and attitudes*, (Belmont, CA: Wadsworth, 1981), 75-80.

[2]Edward T. Hall, *The Hidden Dimension* (New York, Anchor Books, 1990), 116-125.

GROWING AS A LEADER

LEARNING

FINANCIAL SAVVY

FUTURES THINKING

SKILLS & EXPERIENCE

CAREER RELATIONSHIPS

LEADERSHIP LEARNING PLAN

"What got you here won't get you there."–Marshall Goldsmith

Purpose
What is my purpose for learning at this time?

Goal
What do I want or need to learn to be the leader I want to be?

What strengths do I want to develop further?

What am I most interested in learning?

How can I obtain and respond to good developmental feedback?

What must I learn to be more effective in my current or future roles?

What learning do trends and the employment outlook suggest?

Development Areas
Skills:

Why I Want to Learn This:

Learning Questions:

Learning Methods

For best results, incorporate active methods.

How do I learn best?

What formal learning options are available to me?
(e.g., classes, training, coaching)

What informal learning options are available?
(e.g., observation, interviewing, networking, asking for feedback and advice, researching, reading)

What active methods can I incorporate into my learning plan?
(e.g., projects, experiences, applications, teaching others, volunteering, experimenting, demonstration, simulation)

Success

What I will be able to demonstrate or do as a result of my learning:

Benefits to me/Benefits to others:

How I will evaluate my progress:

Resources & Support
What resources and support do I need to carry out my plan:

Timing
I'll start ...

I'll finish by ...

To achieve this, I'll schedule ...

Checkpoints along the way:

Maintaining Momentum
How I'll keep my learning goal and process top-of-mind:

Possible obstacles or challenges:

How I'll handle them:

FINANCIAL SAVVY

How does money flow through your organization? Draw a "Money Map."

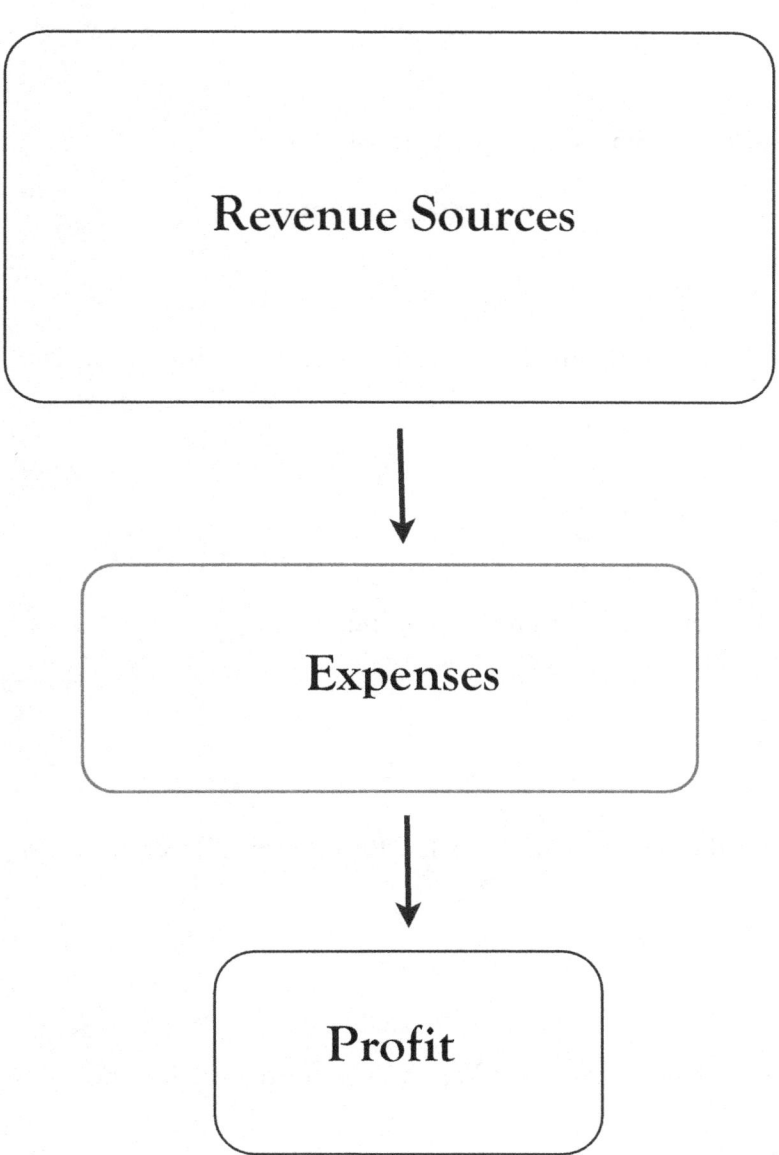

Where does the **Revenue** come from in your organization? List the top sources.

Top Products/Services:

Top Customers/Revenue Contributors:

Where does the **Profit** come from in your organization? List the top sources.

Where are Revenues and Profits **growing?**

Where are the **opportunities** for new Revenue and Revenue growth?

What are the most significant **Expenses** your organization incurs?

Where are the financial **challenges**?

What financial **risks** exist for your organization?

What areas are **vulnerable** to cuts?

What are the most critical financial **metrics** to watch?

Your Cost to the Organization (Salary + 25-35% for Benefits):

Your Contribution/Value to the Organization:

How could you increase your Value?

TUNE INTO TRENDS

Leaders need to be a step ahead. Watch for opportunities for progress and growth in your field and career, as well as signals and drivers of disruption. Set up a system to monitor key trends and record ideas and opportunities to research further.

Information Sources To Monitor
(news sources, websites, blogs, reports)

Trends to Watch

Go For Growth!

Growth Industries to Watch

Growth Organizations

Growth Roles and Jobs

Imagine the Future

"In dealing with the future, it is far more important to be imaginative than to be right "— Alvin Toffler, *Future Shock*

Signals of Change

"A signal is a specific example of the future in the present."—Marina Gorbis

Patterns or Major Drivers Causing Changes

Possible Implications

Possible Change Scenarios

Potential Opportunities

DEVELOP SKILLS FOR THE LONG HAUL

The rapid change of this era demands continual learning. Technology skills will require timely updating and upgrading. While this will sometimes seem to be the most urgent learning need, be sure to invest in other essential skills for the long haul as well.

Here is a list of ten timeless "power skills" that will help you leverage your expertise and other skills. Invest in developing and updating these skills for new technology and the times.

10 Timeless "Power Skills"

Communication & Presentation
Influence
Negotiation
Strategic Thinking
Financial Savvy
Tech Savvy
Team & Talent Development
Creativity & Innovation
Learning
Personal Productivity

Skills for the Future

Additionally, three categories of skills rise in priority along with the technological developments of this era.

Technology Skills
Emerging technologies will continue to drive change and opportunity. Technology Specialists will need to continually upgrade existing skills and learn to work with new technologies. The rest of us, Technology

Competents, will learn to use new technologies to improve our productivity and expand applications in our fields.

Human Skills

As more work will be accomplished through technology-enabled means, uniquely human skills will be critical to moving and connecting people and ideas, creating meaning, and operating successfully in a new era. I refer to these as "the New Seven Cs": Critical Thinking, Communication, Collaboration, Creativity, Change, Coaching, and Caring.

Career Skills

The rapid change of this era will lead to shifts in the career landscape. New careers will emerge as others fade. There's likely to be more mobility in careers. Employers may have a greater choice of employees for roles that don't require a physical presence. Workers may make different choices based on personal values and needs. As employers seek more flexibility in meeting demand, more workers may be "free agents." Continual career reinvention is likely to be a factor for many. It's hard to predict exactly what this will look like, but strong Career Management Skills, such as Learning, Self-Knowledge, Personal Productivity, Networking, and Career Communication, will provide an advantage as we navigate future career paths.

SKILLS STRATEGY

What skills will be required for your target career position?

Which "Power Skills" could you develop and leverage?

Which "Skills for the Future" would be most beneficial?

For what Specialization would you most like to be known?

What steps can you take to acquire and practice these skills?

ADD NEW EXPERIENCES

Consider ways to add to your professional "bag of tricks" by acquiring new and different experiences. Listed below are examples of high-growth experiences. What could you do to:

Start something

Create a new revenue source

Fix something

Solve a problem

Do something different

Participate in a cross-functional team

Lead a project

Lead a change

Take a calculated risk

Lead an outside project

Experience a different culture

Innovate

NEXT-LEVEL CHALLENGES

As you advance to take on higher-level challenges, you may find they involve:

- Greater reach and impact
- More complex problems
- Higher expectations
- Greater visibility
- Greater emphasis on results
- Larger opportunities
- Bigger risks
- Greater dependency on others
- Longer time-horizon
- More ambiguity
- More challenging politics
- Greater reliance on "soft" skills
- Less likelihood of getting "straight" information
- Less likelihood of getting honest feedback
- Greater distance from "the front line"
- A greater level of commitment

What types of shift in thinking will you need to make?

SUPPORT NETWORKS

"We deceive ourselves when we fancy that only weakness needs support.
Strength needs it far more."
- Madame Swetchine

As our world becomes more complex and fast-paced, we need each other more than ever.

Support can take many different forms. For example, support can be demonstrated as:
- Friendship
- Practical advice or help
- Financial or physical resources
- Information
- Sponsorship
- Attentive confidential listening
- Respectful and honest feedback
- Reinforcement and encouragement
- Inspiration
- Appreciation

Since we need different types of support at different times and under different circumstances, an effective support network will include various types of individuals—family, friends, professionals, colleagues, community members, etc.—and keep growing as we do.

Lasting relationships that provide support are two-way. As you develop your support network, remember that effective support is usually reciprocal, although it might take different forms. For instance, you might provide practical advice or information to someone in your network, and they might act as a sounding board for you. Providing sincere support to others as a regular practice makes it easier to ask for and receive support when needed.

Ask yourself:
- *What kinds of support do you most need?*
- *Whom can you turn to for support?*
- *Who can turn to you?*
- *What types of support can you provide to others?*

When seeking support, consider the other's time and needs. Some suggestions:
- Be clear on what it is you want. Prepare a request or question. For example:
  - *I'd like your opinion/advice on ...*
  - *I'm looking for ... Who do you know who might ...?*
- Express appreciation. If appropriate, be prepared to offer something in return.
- Follow up: Let them know what happened as a result of their support.

FINDING A MENTOR

Mentor: an experienced and trusted advisor

Successful people often acknowledge the role a mentor or mentors played in their success. What's sometimes puzzling, though, is how to find a mentor.

Historically, career mentor relationships were often informal "let me show you the ropes" relationships between people of similar backgrounds. Older managers found satisfaction in helping younger versions of themselves. The mentor "chose" the mentee. While this is still one type of mentor relationship, today mentorship encompasses a much broader range of participants, relationships, and formats. Types of mentor relationships include:

Peer-To-Peer Mentorships
In this type of mentor relationship, peers in similar roles collaborate to raise overall performance by sharing best practices and collaborating to solve problems.
- Approach: *"Are you seeing what I'm seeing?"*, *"How have you handled x?"*, *"What has worked for you in y situation?"*
- Peers might be within the same organization or, if appropriate, individuals with similar roles in different organizations.
- Format: This form of mentoring ranges from individual relationships to support groups communicating regularly in person or through social media, conference calls, or Internet groups.

"Fill in the gaps" Mentoring
As our world becomes more complex, it's hard to know everything. Cross-pollination carries many benefits. In this type of mentorship, one seeks out others with knowledge and experience in different areas. For example, a Technical Manager might seek another manager with financial, marketing, or specialized technical expertise.
- Approach: *"I'm looking to broaden my knowledge of the business. Would you be willing to share your perspective with me? I'd like to see the business through your eyes."*

- Format: The parties might meet one or more times, ask and answer questions, share perspectives, and agree to be available as needed in the future.

"Reverse" Mentorships

Instead of a more experienced person mentoring a younger, less-experienced person, the younger person might act as the mentor.

- Example: A "Baby Boomer" manager seeks out someone from a younger generation to get perspective (and sometimes tech advice!).

Formal Mentor Programs

A company, industry, or educational organization often sponsors these programs. A less-experienced manager is typically paired up with a higher-level executive for a year-long structured program, often pairing people who would not otherwise know each other well. Some structure (e.g., guidelines, materials, possibly training) is typically provided.

Informal Mentoring

This type of mentor relationship usually evolves where a higher-level, more experienced mentor and their mentee have developed a rapport based on a shared experience, such as a common background or interest, membership in an organization, or a former boss/subordinate relationship. The mentor might guide the mentee and be available as a sounding board either occasionally or regularly.

Self-Initiated Mentorship

Here, a less-experienced manager seeks out a more-experienced manager (usually not in a direct reporting line) and asks them to act as a mentor.

- Tips if you choose to pursue this: Respect the mentor's time. Have a clear purpose. Propose a structure the mentor is likely to be able to agree to. Be flexible. Be willing to commit and to contribute. Be appreciative. Give back.

Criteria for a Successful Mentorship Relationship

When looking for a mentor relationship, consider the following essential criteria:

- **Good "fit":** The parties feel a sense of rapport and enjoy being with each other.
- **Commitment:** Both parties are willing and able to commit the necessary time and energy to the relationship.
- **Structure:** The structure is defined and agreeable to both parties (e.g., how often, when, and how they will be in touch)
- **Mutual Benefit:** The relationship is two-way. Both parties gain something from it.
- **Professional Appropriateness:** The relationship doesn't create an uncomfortable or unethical situation for either party.

Exploring Options

Questions to consider when exploring your mentorship options:

- *What do you want to learn? From whom could you learn that?*
- *What type of relationship do you want?*
- *What do you bring to the relationship?*
- *What structure is likely to work best?*

Action Steps:

1) Determine your objectives.
2) Identify possibilities for mentorship.
3) Approach a potential mentor or group.
4) Propose and negotiate an arrangement that works for all parties involved.
5) Carry out the mentorship plan.
6) Give back. Who might benefit from your mentorship?

Made in the USA
Monee, IL
07 January 2024

51355297R00092